THE CITY LIBRARY
SPRINGFIELD, (MA) CITY LIBRARY

DISCARDED BY
THE CITY LIBRARY

Emily's
Place for
Children

MAR 1 1 2021

Mineraloids

by Grace Hansen

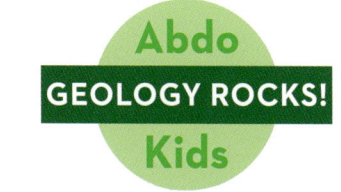

Abdo Kids Jumbo is an Imprint of Abdo Kids
abdobooks.com

abdobooks.com

Published by Abdo Kids, a division of ABDO, P.O. Box 398166, Minneapolis, Minnesota 55439.
Copyright © 2020 by Abdo Consulting Group, Inc. International copyrights reserved in all countries.
No part of this book may be reproduced in any form without written permission from the publisher.
Abdo Kids Jumbo™ is a trademark and logo of Abdo Kids.

Printed in the United States of America, North Mankato, Minnesota.

052019
092019

Photo Credits: iStock, Shutterstock

Production Contributors: Teddy Borth, Jennie Forsberg, Grace Hansen
Design Contributors: Dorothy Toth, Pakou Moua

Library of Congress Control Number: 2018963345
Publisher's Cataloging-in-Publication Data

Names: Hansen, Grace, author.
Title: Mineraloids / by Grace Hansen.
Description: Minneapolis, Minnesota : Abdo Kids, 2020 | Series: Geology rocks!
    set 2 | Includes online resources and index.
Identifiers: ISBN 9781532185595 (lib. bdg.) | ISBN 9781532186578 (ebook) |
    ISBN 9781532187063 (Read-to-me ebook)
Subjects: LCSH: Gems--Juvenile literature. | Precious stones--Juvenile literature. |
    Rocks--Identification--Juvenile literature. | Geology--Juvenile literature.
Classification: DDC 549--dc23

Table of Contents

Mineraloids 4

Low-Temperature Mineraloids . . . 8

Impact Mineraloids 12

Volcanic Mineraloids 18

Mineraloid Review 22

Glossary 23

Index 24

Abdo Kids Code 24

Mineraloids

Mineraloids are similar to **minerals** in many ways. They can even look a bit like them. But minerals are **crystalline**. Mineraloids are not.

Mineraloids occur naturally.

They are also very beautiful!

Low-Temperature Mineraloids

Most mineraloids form in low temperatures and pressures. They can form on Earth's surface or below it. Opal is a mineraloid. With the help of water, it forms within Earth's cracks.

Limonite often forms with the help of water and iron-rich **minerals**.

Impact Mineraloids

Some mineraloids form from large impacts. When an **asteroid** strikes, it flash-melts everything around it. Things cool down quite quickly afterward. This can form new things.

Moldavite is an impact glass. It was formed 15 million years ago. Then, an **asteroid** struck the area that is now Eastern Europe.

15

Libyan Desert glass formed after an **asteroid** strike around 29 million years ago. It can be found in the desert between Egypt and Libya.

Volcanic Mineraloids

Some mineraloids form from **magma**. If magma cools too quickly, it does not have time to form crystals. It can harden into volcanic glass. Obsidian is a black, smooth volcanic glass.

19

Pumice is a volcanic glass that is rough. It forms from **magma** in explosive eruptions. It cools so quickly that gas bubbles stay trapped inside.

21

Mineraloid Review

Impact Mineraloids	Volcanic Mineraloids	Low-Temperature Mineraloids
 Libyan Desert glass	 obsidian	 chrysocolla
 moldavite	 Pele's tears	 limonite
 tektites	 pumice	 opal

Glossary

asteroid – a small, rocky, planet-like body that circles the sun. It can sometimes be pulled out of orbit and collide with planets, like Earth.

crystalline – having the structure and form of a crystal.

magma – hot, liquid matter beneath earth's surface that cools to form igneous rock. These rocks can also be considered mineraloids.

mineral – a substance, like gold, silver, and iron, formed in the earth that is not of an animal or plant.

pressure – a steady force upon something.

Index

asteroid 12, 14, 16

Eastern Europe 14

Egypt 16

formation 8, 10, 12, 16, 18, 20

iron 10

Libya 16

Libyan Dessert glass 16

limonite 10

minerals 4, 10

moldavite 14

obsidian 18

opal 8

pumice 20

volcanoes 18, 20

water 8, 10

Visit **abdokids.com** to access crafts, games, videos, and more!

Use Abdo Kids code **GMK5595** or scan this QR code!

24